CATS SET V
The Designer Cats

SAFARI CATS

Jill C. Wheeler
ABDO Publishing Company

visit us at
www.abdopublishing.com

Published by ABDO Publishing Company, 8000 West 78th Street, Edina, Minnesota 55439. Copyright © 2011 by Abdo Consulting Group, Inc. International copyrights reserved in all countries. No part of this book may be reproduced in any form without written permission from the publisher. The Checkerboard Library™ is a trademark and logo of ABDO Publishing Company.

Printed in the United States of America, North Mankato, Minnesota.
092010
012011

 PRINTED ON RECYCLED PAPER

Cover Photo: Photo by Helmi Flick
Interior Photos: Animals Animals p. 19; Getty Images p. 7; Photo by Helmi Flick pp. 9, 11, 13, 17, 18; Photolibrary pp. 5, 15, 21

Series Coordinator: Heidi M.D. Elston
Editors: Heidi M.D. Elston, Megan M. Gunderson
Cover & Interior Design: Neil Klinepier
Production Layout: Jaime Martens

Library of Congress Cataloging-in-Publication Data

Wheeler, Jill C., 1964-
  Safari cats / Jill C. Wheeler.
     p. cm. -- (Cats. Set V, Designer cats)
  Includes bibliographical references and index.
  ISBN 978-1-60453-731-4 (alk. paper)
  1. Safari cat--Juvenile literature. I. Title.
  SF449.S24W44 2010
  636.8--dc22
                                    2009021149

Thinking about a Designer Cat?
Some communities have laws that regulate hybrid animal ownership. Be sure to check with your local authorities before buying a hybrid kitten.

CONTENTS

WILD ABOUT CATS

The first cats to live with humans were actually wildcats. Today, many cat lovers still want pets with a touch of the wild. This wish led to the **breeding** of designer, or **hybrid**, cats. The result is cats that look like wildcats without having all the wild habits.

There are about 37 cat species in the world today. All cats are members of the same animal family. That is the family **Felidae**. Members of this family are called felids. All of them are carnivores.

Felids are native to Africa, Asia, Europe, and North and South America. One felid native to South America is the Geoffroy's cat. Some people keep these wildcats as pets. Others breed Geoffroy's cats with **domestic** cats. This creates a hybrid cat called the safari. The safari is one of the rarest designer cats.

Domestic cats share their beginnings with the big and small wildcats of the world.

Geoffroy's Cats

The Geoffroy's cat is a small South American wildcat. It occupies a variety of **habitats** in Bolivia, Argentina, Paraguay, and Brazil. The Geoffroy's cat is the most common small wildcat in its range.

This small cat weighs from 6 to 10 pounds (3 to 5 kg). It stands 6 to 10 inches (15 to 25 cm) tall. And, it is 9 to 15 inches (23 to 38 cm) long.

The color of the Geoffroy's cat varies depending on location. The coat can be black to silver gray to deep orange. All Geoffroy's cats are covered in spots.

The Geoffroy's cat is a good climber, swimmer, and hunter. It eats birds, frogs, fish, **rodents**, insects, and small lizards.

Keeping the Geoffroy's cat as a pet requires permits. And because it is a wild animal, the Geoffroy's cat needs special handling. It often does not do well with children or strangers. An alternative pet may be the safari cat.

The Geoffroy's cat hunts at night and sleeps in trees during the day.

CREATING SAFARIS

The safari cat is a rare **hybrid**. This is due to the difficulty in **breeding** them. **Domestic** cats have 38 **chromosomes**, while Geoffroy's cats have just 36. It is very difficult to breed two species that have different chromosome numbers.

The effect of this difference is that first generation (F1) safari kittens carry 37 chromosomes. This seems to greatly increase size. F1 safaris are much larger than their parents.

Geoffroy's cats and house cats have other differences, too. Geoffroy's cats carry their young for 72 to 78 days. Domestic cats give birth 63 to 65 days after mating. Most safari kittens are born early by wildcat standards. So, humans may need to provide constant care to the tiny, helpless kittens.

An F1 female safari may be **bred** for kittens. Yet most male safaris are **sterile**. So, breeders look to other spotted, **domestic** male cats. The father is usually an Egyptian mau, a Bengal cat, or an ocicat.

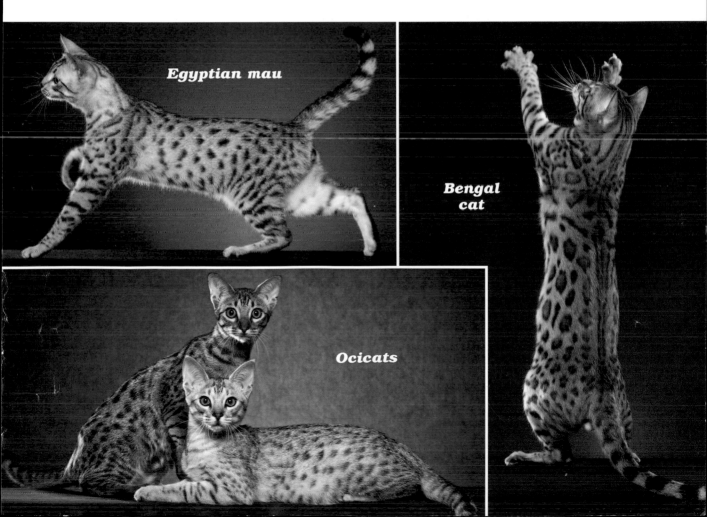

Egyptian mau

Bengal cat

Ocicats

A Rare Hybrid

It is believed the safari cat was first **bred** in the 1970s. Yet, it is estimated there are fewer than 100 safaris in the United States today. Most of these are F1 safaris. Only a few second and third generation safaris exist. Still, there are many breeders working hard to advance this **hybrid**.

The safari has not become as popular as other designer cats. This is likely because of the difficulty in breeding this hybrid. As a result, the safari is one of the rarest designer cats.

Because they are so rare, safari cats are expensive. People who want one can expect to pay anywhere from $5,000 to $12,000!

Some people call the safari the "Rolls Royce" of hybrid cats. The Rolls Royce is a very expensive, unusual car.

SAFARI CATS

Imagine a 25-pound (11-kg) spotted house cat with the face of a wildcat. This **domestic** cat has small, rounded ears and big eyes. It also has a broad head and a wide nose. That is a good description of a safari cat.

The safari cat is an affectionate pet. Unlike the Geoffroy's cat, it is good with children and even strangers.

Like most **hybrid** cats, the safari loves to play. And, it needs a lot of time with its human owners. This fun-loving cat wants to be in its owner's lap. It may even perch on its owner's head!

Many owners claim the safari shows more affection than other hybrid cats.

BEHAVIOR

Like many **hybrid** cats, safaris have a lot of energy! They are usually on the move, running and climbing. Safaris are not for people who want couch potato pets. They demand a lot of attention from their owners.

Safaris are also very intelligent. Safari owners report that their cats will use their front paws like hands. They can pick up objects and even open things!

Like common house cats, safaris are generally easy to train to use a **litter box**. Many owners also say their safaris act more like dogs than house cats. This is true of many hybrid cats.

Cats need to chase, pounce, and bat at objects to keep out of mischief.

Coats & Colors

Like the Geoffroy's cat, the safari displays a striking coat. Its color and markings make it a beautiful pet.

The safari comes in three different colors. The coat can be gold with black spots. It can be black with darker black spots. Or, the safari can have a silver base coat with black markings. However, that is more unusual.

The safari's markings may look like paw prints. Or they may be rosettes. These spots have at least two colors or shades in them.

The safari's coat color and pattern depend on its parents.

SIZES

Safari cats are among the largest **hybrid** cats. There are reports from the 1970s of males weighing 36 pounds (16 kg)!

Since this hybrid was first **bred**, few males have been produced. Generally, adult males can reach 25 pounds (11 kg). Female safari cats are smaller than males. However, fully grown females can still tip the scales at around 18 pounds (8 kg).

The more wild blood there is in a safari, the larger it is. The species of each parent also affects the size of the kitten.

A domestic father, such as the ocicat, tends to create smaller kittens.

A Geoffroy's cat father will likely create larger kittens.

CARE

More than anything, safari cats need attention from their human owners. They are active and like to play.

Like all **domestic** cats, safaris need regular care from a veterinarian. A veterinarian can provide **vaccines**. He or she can also **spay** or **neuter** safari kittens.

Safari cats do fine on a regular diet of dry cat food. However, their wild side still likes fresh meat. Safari owners must not leave the meat out too long. Otherwise, it will spoil. In addition, safari cats need plenty of fresh water each day.

Safari cats are quite rare. So, no one knows for sure how long they are likely to live. However, it is believed they will live about 15 years. With lots of love, safari cats will make fun-loving family members.

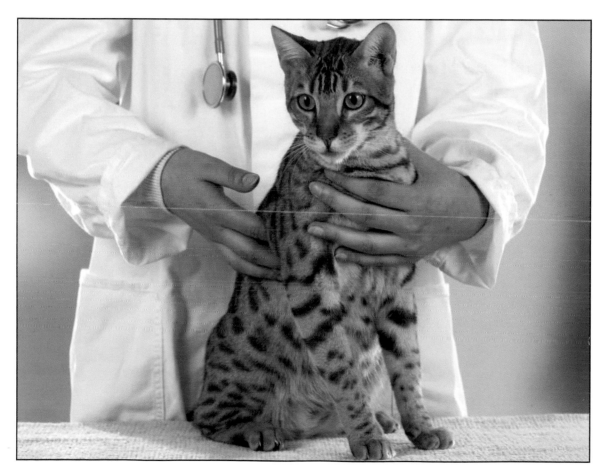

A veterinarian can help your pet maintain good health.

GLOSSARY

breed - a group of animals sharing the same ancestors and
appearance. A breeder is a person who raises animals.
Raising animals is often called breeding them.

chromosome - a tiny, thin, threadlike structure found in
cells of all organisms. Chromosomes carry the physical
or behavioral features offspring receive from parents.
The passing of such features is called heredity.

domestic - tame, especially relating to animals.

Felidae (FEHL-uh-dee) - the scientific Latin name for the cat
family. Members of this family are called felids. They
include domestic cats, lions, tigers, leopards, jaguars,
cougars, wildcats, lynx, and cheetahs.

habitat - a place where a living thing is naturally found.

hybrid - an offspring of two animals or plants of different
races, breeds, varieties, species, or genera.

litter box - a box filled with cat litter, which is similar to
sand. Cats use litter boxes to dispose of their waste.

neuter (NOO-tuhr) - to remove a male animal's reproductive organs.

rodent - any of several related animals that have large front teeth for gnawing. Common rodents include mice, squirrels, and beavers.

spay - to remove a female animal's reproductive organs.

sterile - unable to produce offspring.

vaccine (vak-SEEN) - a shot given to animals or humans to prevent them from getting an illness or a disease.

WEB SITES

To learn more about safari cats, visit ABDO Publishing Company online. Web sites about safari cats are featured on our Book Links page. These links are routinely monitored and updated to provide the most current information available.

www.abdopublishing.com

INDEX